All praise be Yours, my Lord, through... mother, Who feeds us in her s... various fruits and colored flo... be Yours, my Lord, through... love of You; Through those... ...d trial.

Happy those who endure in peace, For by You, Most High, they will be crowned. All praise be Yours, my Lord, through Sister Death, From whose embrace no mortal can escape. Woe to those who die in mortal sin! Happy those she finds doing Your holy will! The second death can do no harm to them.

Praise and bless my Lord, and give thanks And serve Him with great humility.

THE PRAYER OF SAINT FRANCIS

Lord make me an instrument of Your peace.
Where there is hatred, let me sow love;
Where there is injury, pardon;
Where there is doubt, faith;
Where there is despair, hope;
Where there is darkness, light;
Where there is sadness, joy.

O Lord, grant that I may not so much seek
To be consoled as to console;
To be understood as to understand;
To be loved as to love.

For it is in giving that we receive;
It is in pardoning that we are pardoned;
And it is in dying that we are born to
eternal life.

AMEN

SAINT FRANCIS

OF

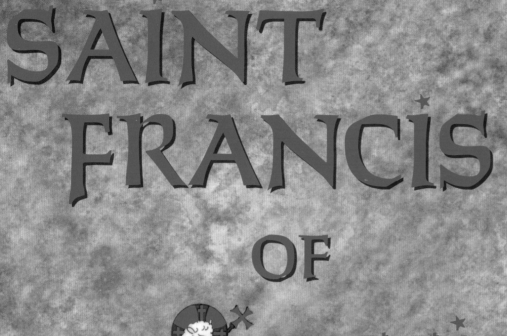

ASSISI

Written and Illustrated by

DEMI

Wisdom Tales

Saint Francis of Assisi
©Demi, 2012

Book design by Stephen Williams

Wisdom Tales is an imprint of World Wisdom, Inc.

For Grazia Gotti

Library of Congress Cataloging-in-Publication Data

Demi.
  Saint Francis of Assisi / written and illustrated by Demi.
     p. cm.
  ISBN 978-1-937786-04-5 (casebound : alk. paper) I. Francis, of Assisi, Saint, 1182-1226--Juvenile literature. 2. Christian saints--Italy--Assisi--Biography--Juvenile literature. I. Title.
  BX4700.F6D3995 2012
  271'.302--dc23
  [B]

                                        2012010725

Illustrations are rendered in mixed media

Printed in China on acid-free paper
Production Date: May, 2012 Plant & Location: Printed by Everbest Printing (Guangzhou, China), Co. Ltd
Job / Batch: 107904

For information address Wisdom Tales,
P.O. Box 2682, Bloomington, Indiana 47402-2682
www.wisdomtalespress.com

In the days when medieval knights fought for glory and musicians sang of love and honor, a little boy was born in a stable in Assisi, Italy in 1182. His mother was Mona Pica, a deeply religious woman. His father Pietro Bernardone was a wealthy cloth merchant.

From the start Francis was generous, brilliant, and brave. As a boy he loved fine horses and playing with his friends, among whom he was always the leader. As he grew older, Francis dressed in beautiful clothes and joined the feasts and banquets of wealthy sons of noblemen. There he was always the life of the party.

Francis and his friends dreamed of glory and battle. They sang songs to the lute, and ate, drank, and danced all through the night, dreaming of fame.

When Assisi went to war with the nearby city of Perugia, Francis and his friends were overjoyed. Now was their time for fame and glory! In a brand new suit of shining armor that his father had bought for him, Francis rode proudly off to war.

But along the way he saw a knight whose rusty armor was falling apart. Francis felt so sorry for the knight, and so troubled that he might cause him any jealousy, that he jumped off his horse and gave his entire suit of shining armor to the poor knight.

Francis fought heroically, but he was captured and thrown into a dark prison. There he saw rich knights and poor soldiers die side by side, and began wondering whether there was any glory in war. It all seemed so empty and foolish. He comforted the prisoners with song and lifted their spirits with jokes and laughter.

After one year his father ransomed him, and Francis returned home a hero.

B ut suddenly Francis fell ill with a dangerously high fever. Lying in bed, Francis dreamed he saw swords and shields in the shape of a cross. He thought this meant he should fight for the Pope, for the Pope was calling on knights to fight for Christianity.

As soon as Francis recovered he joined the Pope's war against the German king. But God didn't want Francis to be an earthly knight. He wanted Francis to be a heavenly one. He struck Francis down with a sickness that made him fall from his horse, and sent him a message telling him to serve God and not men.

So Francis went home and began to pray in the mountains alone. One day he received a glorious vision of Jesus suffering on the cross. Love and sincere longing for the simple life of Jesus overcame him, and he began helping the sick and the poor.

Another day Francis met a leper on the road. Although he had been a fearless knight in battle, he was frightened by the leper's bleeding wounds and missing fingers. But instead of turning away, with great courage and compassion, Francis hugged the poor leper. As he did so a great happiness flooded his whole being. Glowing with joy, he rode to the leper colony asking forgiveness, giving them clothes and money, and hugging and kissing them all.

Francis often went to pray for Divine guidance in a little ruined church called San Damiano. One day, while inside the church, Christ on the cross spoke to him. "Francis, go and repair my church, which as you see is falling into ruins." Francis gave a bag of his father's money to help repair the little church. He also gave away his father's best silks to clothe the poor.

His father was furious. He dragged Francis before the Bishop of Assisi saying, "This wicked son stole from the father that has given him everything on earth!" Francis said, "You are no longer my father!" Then he tore every piece of clothing from his body. Completely naked, he turned to his father and said, "Here are the earthly clothes you have given me. From now on, I will obey only my Father in Heaven!"

B arefoot and dressed in a hermit's robe with only a rope around his waist, Francis began begging for food, singing as he went. Now that he owned nothing, he felt richer. The sun was his brother; the moon was his sister.

P eople gave him bread and
asked what more he needed.
"Stones!" said Francis, "to
build the churches of Heaven!"
Francis then rebuilt the little
church of San Damiano and two
other churches. On February 24,
1209 the Holy Spirit revealed
to Francis the life of poverty to
which God was calling him.

A very wealthy nobleman named Bernard joined Francis in his life of poverty and service to others. For guidance Francis opened the Bible three times. There he read, "Go sell what you have and give it to the poor." "Do not keep gold or silver or money in your purse, nor wallet for your journey, and only one pair of sandals and a single tunic." "If anyone wishes to come to me, let him deny himself and take up the cross and follow me."

That very day Bernard sold all of his possessions and donated them to the poor. Peter Catani and Giles, a farmer, next joined Francis.

Soon there were twelve brothers. Unlike other monks in monasteries, they lived like beggars in the open air, never knowing where they would eat or sleep next. Once, at a crossroads, a brother asked Francis where to go next. Holding his shoulders, Francis spun him around like a top until he stopped. "There you shall go!" said Francis. "The road you're facing now is the right road, for God has shown this to you!"

Francis called his followers the Friars Minor, or Lesser Brothers. Forgetting all earthly glory, they were to be brothers to all men, humble yet cheerful, peaceful, simple, and pure.

Francis wrote a simple Rule for his brothers based on the Gospels. He traveled to Rome with his brothers to get the formal approval of Pope Innocent III to go forth and preach as Jesus had done. The brothers who lived in peace and poverty didn't spend much time washing themselves. When the Pope saw their muddy, stained clothes he said, "Go roll with the pigs! That is all you are fit for!"

Francis went out and found a pigsty. He said, "Brother pig may I join you?" and he rolled in the sty. He then went back to the Pope even muddier. The Pope held his nose, but blessed Francis anyway, because the poverty of Francis was a lesson even for the Pope.

The twelve brothers returned to Assisi and lived in great poverty in a simple shed. Soon, however, more and more brothers joined them, and they had to move to a larger home in a church. A beautiful and noble girl named Clare wanted to join Francis. His words of God enlightened her heart, and his works seemed divine. One Friday she found Francis at a wayside inn, waiting for his fish dinner. The innkeeper was a mean man who knew that on Fridays Christians could only eat fish, but served Francis chicken. Francis humbly received the chicken, then stood up and raising his hand, blessed the chicken—which instantly turned into a beautiful plump fish! Clare's faith was sealed by this miracle!

When Clare's parents wanted her to marry a rich nobleman she ran away to join the monks. She changed into a nun's tunic and tied a rope around her waist. Francis cut off her beautiful blond hair and covered her head with a black veil. She took vows of poverty, chastity, and obedience, recognizing Francis as her superior. This was the beginning of the nun's order of the Poor Clares. It was also the beginning of Clare's journey to becoming a saint.

The gentle love and charity of Francis extended to everything in the universe. If he accidentally kicked a stone, he apologized to it. If a worm was on the road, he saved its life. If wild bees were hungry in winter he brought them warm wine and honey to eat.

One day Francis preached to the birds: "My sister birds, you owe God great gratitude, and should always praise Him. Praise Him because you can fly so freely wherever you please, and for your most beautiful coat of feathers, and for the food you do not have to work for, and for the lovely voices your Creator has given you."

Francis continued, "God gives you rivers and springs to drink from, and hills and mountains, cliffs and rocks in which to hide and high trees to build your nests in. And though you neither spin nor weave, He gives you and your young ones necessary clothing. Therefore you must greatly love your Creator since He has given you such blessings."

Instantly the little birds opened their beaks and sang a wonderful song, then bowed to the earth praising the Lord. Francis blessed them, making a sign of the cross. Then all the birds flew up in the sky forming the sign of the cross, and singing the word of God.

One brother named Anthony went to the sea and called, "You fishes of the sea, listen to the word of God!" And all of a sudden large and small fishes gathered before him and held their heads high above the water so they could hear. Like a beautiful colored carpet the fish arranged themselves in perfect order. The biggest fish at the back and the smallest in front.

Anthony said further, "Brother fishes, you should give as many thanks as you can to your Creator who has granted you such a dwelling place. He has given you many places to hide from storms. He has given you fins, so you can swim wherever you wish, and He has given you His blessing, so you should praise and bless the Lord." The fish opened their mouths and nodded their heads. They then praised God as they could, swimming, diving, rolling, and jumping with joy in every direction.

Francis tamed everything he met—even a dangerous wolf who was killing sheep and people in the town of Gubbio. The town gates were shut tight as everyone was too terrified to go out. Francis armed himself with only his great faith and went out to meet the wolf. From the edge of the forest the wolf came running, baring all his sharp teeth. Francis made the sign of the cross, and with the power of God, stopped the wolf right in its tracks. Then Francis called to the wolf, "Come to me brother wolf. In the name of Christ I order you not to hurt me or anyone else." The wolf closed its terrible jaws, lowered its head, and lay down at Francis' feet just like a lamb.

Together the wolf and Francis walked back to Gubbio to the great astonishment of everyone. Francis said to the people, "Here is brother wolf who has come to say he's sorry." The wolf bowed down before everyone and gave Francis his paw. Then the people of Gubbio greeted the wolf and fed him good food, and they all lived together in gentle peace.

F rancis brought peace to
many Italian cities that were
fighting with each other.

All across the land, everyone sang his praises.

Francis wanted to preach to
the Muslims in Spain and
North Africa. In 1219 Francis
sailed to join the Crusades
in Egypt.

Francis thought, "How much better it would be to preach to the Muslims and conquer them with love rather than to kill them with the sword." At the risk of his life, Francis crossed the warring desert and found the Sultan lying in his great silken tent.

Francis began to preach to the Sultan, "There is only one God. It is wrong for people to make wars in the name of God, each side believing that God is with them alone. Give up all other teachers and learn from Christ who taught men how to love one another." The Sultan could see that Francis was a very holy saint, burning with love for all mankind. But in the name of Allah he was duty-bound to defend his lands and his religion from the Christians. With great admiration he said, "If all Christians were like you, there would be no war between us!" He gave Francis presents and permission to travel safely anywhere in his empire.

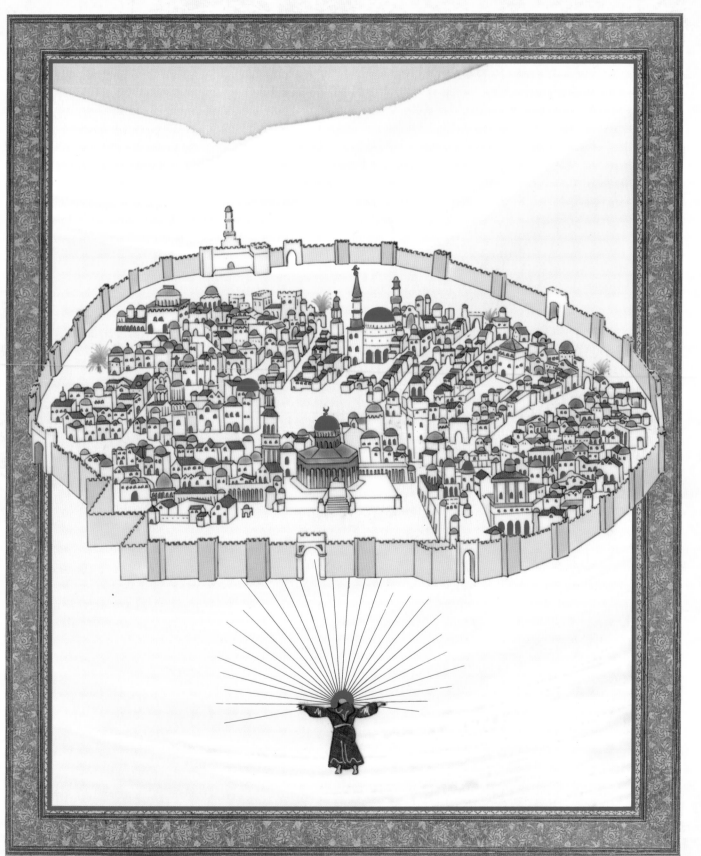

Francis visited Jerusalem and was so overcome with joy that he fell to the ground in prayer.

He also visited Bethlehem, the River Jordan, and Nazareth.

The Franciscan Order was based on poverty, chastity, and obedience, imitating the life of Christ as described in the Gospels. Brothers prayed, preached, worked, and begged, giving up all worldly things in order to live a life closer to Christ.

M any people wanted to join Francis but found the rules too strict. So Francis set up a Third Order which ordinary people of any position, job, or class could join.

F rancis deeply loved Christ's poverty. One Easter he was alarmed to see his brothers preparing rich foods for a fancy feast. Showing his complete disapproval, he sat down on the floor just like a beggar, and ate some stale bread crumbs.

He said, "We, more than anyone else, must follow the example of poverty set by the Son of God." When he saw the rich houses some of the brothers were living in he said, "This money should have been spent building churches and helping the poor."

For many, the rules of absolute poverty were too difficult. But Francis was divinely inspired to reject making the rules any easier. From a mountaintop he shouted, "The rules of poverty must be observed to the letter without gloss, without gloss, without gloss!" But not many could follow.

Finally Francis went to the Pope, who advised him to give in a little, for the Franciscan brothers were learning—but all at different rates.

Francis accepted the wisdom of the Pope's words, but the compromise weighed heavily on his heart. He went to the mountain of La Verna to pray and be alone. There several brothers built him a hut of pine branches.

As soon as Francis began to pray, his prayer was so deep that the whole mountain seemed to light up. The brothers at the bottom said the mountain seemed on fire!

In his prayer, a glowing light began to shine all around him. In that light Francis saw an angel with six shining wings appear before him. And Francis realized it was Christ on the Cross—glowing with love. And he realized by the inner flame of love, he himself was being transformed into Christ on the Cross.

When the vision departed, Francis felt in his heart the living love of God, and his hands and feet and body bore the marks of Christ who had died on the Cross.

Francis wanted everyone to remember the humble birth of Jesus Christ. On Christmas Eve in Greccio in 1223, Francis made a manger filled with hay. He brought in cows and donkeys, sheep and lambs to reconstruct the Nativity scene. At midnight all the people of the village came carrying candles and torches. They lit up the sky, as did the great Star of Bethlehem many years before.

When they saw the holy manger they were filled with wonder, joy, and peace because it looked so real. Francis sang beautiful songs and said, "Look and always remember. He was poor and he was humble."

Today the whole world copies the way Francis first celebrated the birth of baby Jesus on Christmas Day many years ago.

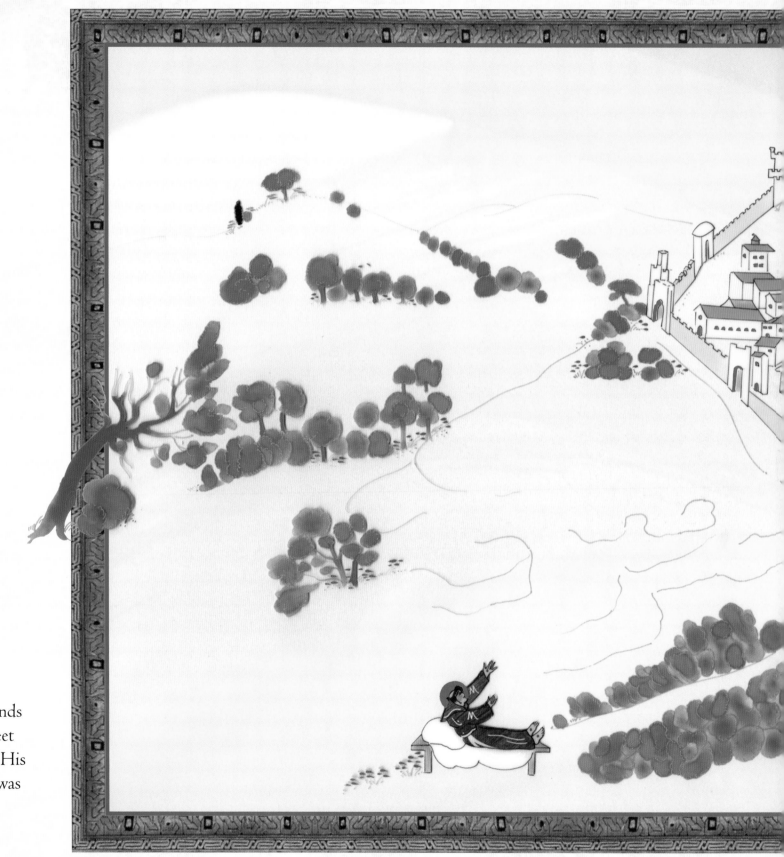

After a time, the wounds on his hands and feet and body would not heal. His eyesight was poor and he was very tired.

F rancis returned home to Assisi, and on the way he blessed the city: "May the Lord bless you, holy city, for through you many souls shall be saved, and in you many servants of God shall dwell, and from you many shall be chosen for the Kingdom of eternal life."

Francis said, "God has forgiven all my sins and promised me the happiness of Paradise. Until I had that revelation, I used to weep over death and over my sins. But after He spoke to me, I have been so filled with joy that I remain in bliss all the time. That is why I sing to the Lord, who has given me His Grace."

On October 3, 1226 Francis joined the blessed in Paradise. Many brothers saw his most holy soul freed from his body and received into the light of heaven. They saw it rise over the waters directly into Paradise. They said, "It was like a star, the size of the moon, the brightness of the sun, carried upwards on a little white cloud."

Two years later, in 1228, Francis was proclaimed a saint by Pope Gregory IX. Next to Christ, Saint Francis remains the most popular saint of all time.

May the Lord bless you and keep you.

May the Lord show His face to you
and have mercy upon you.

May the Lord turn His countenance
to you and give you peace.

Amen

Praise the Lord.

You are the holy Lord God.

You are love; You are charity; You are wisdom; You are humility; You are patience, fortitude, and prudence, ... security ... rest ... joy and gladness, ... justice and temperance, ... wealth and plenty.

You are beauty, You are gentleness, You are the protector, ... keeper, and defender ... our refuge and strength; ... our faith, hope, and charity.